Original title:
Cosmic Cakewalk

Copyright © 2025 Creative Arts Management OÜ
All rights reserved.

Author: Cassandra Whitaker
ISBN HARDBACK: 978-1-80567-848-9
ISBN PAPERBACK: 978-1-80567-969-1

Celestial Dance of Flavor and Light

In the space where comets spin,
The cupcakes twirl with frosting thin.
Planetary pies in orbit glide,
While sprinkles rain from stars so wide.

Doughnuts leap through asteroid fields,
With chocolate coats as bright as shields.
A Milky Way of marshmallow sweet,
Where planets bounce to a sugary beat.

Interstellar Strides Through Glistening Galaxies

Asteroids with jellies jump and sway,
While gummy bears plot their next ballet.
Cosmic cookies in the nebula churn,
As licorice vines twist and turn.

Stars wiggle in delightful rhyme,
While laughter floats through the fabric of time.
Hopping from moon to marshmallow star,
This interstellar party stretches far!

Whimsical Wands of the Universe

Candy canes wave like wizard sticks,
Casting spells with cosmic tricks.
Lollipops twirl in zero-gravity,
Creating a scene of goofy levity.

Chocolate moons break into a dance,
While space mice join in with a prance.
Galactic giggles echo through the void,
As confectionery chaos is deployed.

Celestial Treats and Starlit Beats

Baking cakes on shooting stars,
With frosting that travels to Mars.
Galactic treats are all the rage,
As each star takes center stage.

Popsicles made of comet streams,
Float through night like sugary dreams.
Join the fun in this sweet parade,
Where laughter and candy are lovingly made.

Rhythmic Showers from Above

Stars drip down like chocolate bars,
The moon spins tales of shiny cars.
Planets dance in a gleeful spin,
While comets twirl—let the fun begin!

Meteor showers rain like sprinkles,
Galaxies giggle with little crinkles.
Life is a party in the night sky,
Where laughter echoes as they fly by!

Serene Steps Across the Cosmos

Floating on clouds of cotton candy,
The universe feels sweet and dandy.
Step by step on stars so bright,
Every leap gives a chuckle and light.

With a bounce across the Milky Way,
Aliens join in the fun and play.
They share jokes with a wink and a whirl,
In this dance, all galaxies twirl!

Celestial Pathways and Dreamscapes

Shooting across a candy-striped lane,
Where daydreams giggle in bright refrain.
Nebulae fluff like pillows in sight,
Every wander feels just right!

Fluffy clouds wear hats of lace,
Dreamers prance in a jovial race.
Each twinkle a chuckle, each star a jest,
In the vastness, there's laughter at best!

Harmonies of Light

Glistening notes float in the night air,
Melodies woven with sparkles and flair.
Jupiter hums a whimsical tune,
While Saturn dances with rings like a boon.

Laughter rings out from black holes near,
A symphony built on joy and cheer.
With every sound, the universe plays,
In this concert of light, we dance and sway!

Radiant Galaxy Promenade

Stars wearing party hats, so bright,
Planets boogie, a joyful sight.
Saturn spins with icy rings,
While comets burst and flip like springs.

Meteorites play tag with grace,
Asteroids dance in endless space.
Neon trails of light and cheer,
Galactic giggles we can hear.

Moonbeams twist in silly ways,
Fueling laughter through the days.
A starlit jive that never ends,
Cosmic fun with interstellar friends.

Twirl around the Milky Way,
In this playground where we sway.
Giggles echo through the vast,
Joyful moments that hold fast.

Cosmic Footprints on Infinity

Walking on stardust, oh what bliss,
Tripping over orbs in a galactic kiss.
Footprints left on moons of cheese,
Laughter flows like a cosmic breeze.

Dancing on rings of swirling light,
Falling into a waltz each night.
Footfalls echo in a jolly way,
As gravity teases, making us sway.

Jumping from planets, what a sight,
Wavy motions take us to new heights.
With every step, we bounce around,
In this universe, joy is found.

Every leap leaves laughter bright,
As spaceships zoom in pure delight.
Silly moments span the sky,
In this playful dance, we fly.

Orbital Odyssey

On a ride through the starry dome,
Where rockets zoom, far from home.
Galaxies swirl in vibrant hues,
As we chuckle, losing our shoes.

Riding orbits, oh what fun,
Chasing rays of that hot sun.
Planets giggle and slide around,
Crafts whirling, what a sound.

Cosmic games of hide and seek,
Comets winking, cheek to cheek.
In spacesuits taking silly bows,
Galactic dance, we'll take our vows.

Every turn offers fresh delight,
With friends above in the dark night.
In this journey, laughter sings,
As joy takes flight on sparkling wings.

Ethereal Tango Among Stars

Stars align for a grand ballet,
Twinkling bodies lead the way.
Floating softly, in a trance,
Echoing laughter in a dance.

Neutron stars with heavy beats,
Swaying gently on cosmic streets.
Moonlit laughter fills the air,
As astral partners glide with flair.

Galactic rumbles, toes in space,
Every twirl brings a smiling face.
In this twinkling, vast expanse,
We share our hearts in cosmic dance.

So let's shimmy in the night,
Underneath the starry light.
In this joyful, endless spin,
Where every laugh is deep within.

Cosmic Strut Through the Void

In the galaxy's grand parade,
Stars wobble, they never fade.
Planets giggle in their dance,
While comets twirl in a merry prance.

Black holes laugh, they spin in glee,
Chasing stardust, wild and free.
Asteroids join the joyful spree,
On a slide made of zero gravity!

With each bounce, the cosmos glows,
As laughter through the starlight flows.
Nebulae wear their brightest smiles,
Glistening in the dark for miles.

Jovians chuckle, Saturn grins wide,
As space dust dances like a wild tide.
Together they strut in a playful line,
Through the void, oh isn't it divine?

Twinkling Tides of the Universe

Waves of light on a cosmic sea,
Sailing ships of probability.
Stars play tag with the moonlit rays,
Dancing in flamboyant ballet.

Galaxies spin like candy on a stick,
While the light-years laugh at their cosmic trick.
A sprinkle of stardust, a scoop of delight,
Floating through blackness, oh what a sight!

Astro-critters with antennae tied,
Wager who'll win this interstellar ride.
And dwarfs in the corners always complain,
That nobody pays them much attention again!

Bubbles of brilliance, they pop and twirl,
Life's a game in this glittering whirl.
With every giggle, the universe sways,
As we surf through the light of a thousand days.

Astronomical Ambles

Planets stroll down the Milky Way,
Stopping for jokes at the star buffet.
Each bright twinkle's a wink that they share,
A light-hearted romp through the cosmic air.

Footloose comets embrace the chill,
As meteorites shout, "What a thrill!"
They skip and glide, oh what a sight,
Painting the sky with giggles of light.

In interstellar parks, they play freeze-tag,
While space-time bends with a snap and a wag.
They delight in the echoes of laughter so bold,
Creating warm tales in the starlit cold.

Jumping on nebulae, slipping on rings,
Swirling around, the joy that it brings.
Each bounce and chuckle pack interplanetary cheer,
A hilarious walk on the galactic sphere!

Celestial Canvas of Creation

Splashes of color across the night,
Galaxies churn in a whimsical flight.
Stars drip laughter like paint from a brush,
Creating a melty, delightful hush.

Planets pop like balloons filled with cheer,
Sprinkling smiles in the atmosphere.
Cosmic artists with wobbly hands,
Create silly shapes in expansive lands.

Nebulas swirl in a ticklish twirl,
While cosmic dust sparkles and swirls.
Each creation sings with a funky beat,
As the universe dances on its colorful feet.

So gather 'round in this grand showcase,
Laugh with the stars in sparkling grace.
In a galaxy where giggles abound,
Joy paints the cosmos all around!

Astral March of the Wanderers

In the sky, we prance and jig,
With twinkling stars, we dance a gig.
Galaxies swirl in a dizzy spin,
As laughing comets join the din.

With moonlit shoes, we tap and glide,
Space balloons bounce, oh what a ride!
Planets giggle in a cheeky spin,
While meteors laugh, and join us in.

Through rainbow trails, we twirl and tease,
Shooting stars freeze, then burst with ease.
Each stomp releases a celestial cheer,
As gravity giggles, losing its fear.

So grab your friends, both near and far,
Let's boogie down with a twinkling star.
In this galactic ball for all to join,
Life's a funny dance, don't be coy!

Cosmic Pas de Deux

Two stars in a playful duet,
Swirl and twirl without a fret.
Sip stardust tea, both sweet and spry,
Laughing nebulae in the sky.

Falling through space, we spin with glee,
Whirling in orbits, just you and me.
With each little hop, we giggle aloud,
While distant galaxies form a crowd.

Planets laugh as we glide so bold,
Dancing through the stardust, oh so cold!
With every leap, we chase the sun,
In this twinkling ballet, oh what fun!

So take my hand, let's glide and sway,
In this cheeky waltz, come play, hooray!
In space's grand stage, we steal the scene,
Forever dancing, light and keen.

Heavenly Tread

On clouds of cotton, we skip and bounce,
Chasing comets with giggles to renounce.
Stars overhead, they cheer and chime,
In this delightful, frolicking mime.

With each step, the universe winks,
As black holes bubble and brightly blink.
A step to the left, then a slide so wide,
Twinkle-toed astronauts turn with pride.

Meteor showers rain confetti bright,
Celebrating this stampede of light.
Galactic giggles echo and spark,
As we shuffle through this stellar park.

So come and dance, leave woes behind,
In this universe, true joy you'll find.
As we caper through the celestial spread,
Let's all rejoice with a heavenly tread!

Stardust Soiree

A party of planets, come one, come all,
With Saturn's rings, we'll dance at the ball.
Galactic confetti flies through the night,
In a whirlwind of laughter, it's pure delight!

The moon blows bubbles, what a sight to see,
While meteors burst with glee, whee!
Cosmic cupcakes, a tasty treat,
Nibbling on starlight, oh so sweet!

With pulsars thumping, we shake and jive,
As drumming quasars help us thrive.
We kick up the dust, let's mess the place,
In this joyful shindig, we're full of grace!

So raise your glasses, toast to the skies,
Under the watch of those twinkling eyes.
In this funny frolic, let all worries sway,
Join the stardust soiree, hip-hip-hooray!

Radiant Revelry in the Cosmos

Dancing comets in the night,
Sprinkling stardust, oh what a sight!
Giggles echo through the dark,
As meteors join in with a spark.

Planets twirl in a sugary bliss,
Chasing tails with a starry kiss.
The moon winks with a jovial grin,
Let the interstellar fun begin!

Sugar Stars and Planetary Pastries

Shooting stars with frosted tips,
Candy comets make wild flips.
Galaxies bake in a cosmic oven,
While alien chefs are really lovin'.

Jupiter's donuts, Saturn's tart,
Nibble moons with a joyful heart.
Licorice rings swirl and sway,
In the galaxy's grand buffet!

Twilight Tastes of the Universe's Bounty

Crumbly asteroids roll and bounce,
Tasting nebulae, one can pounce!
Sunbeams drizzle cosmic cream,
On all treats, it's a foodie dream.

Black hole brownies, dark and rich,
Mars made of mousse, what a pitch!
Whimsical waves of sweet delight,
Nibbling stardust in the night!

A Pastry Parade Across the Milky Way

Join the march of tasty treats,
Checkered flags, oh the sweets!
Chocolate meteors zoom by fast,
In this fest, good times are cast.

Frosted galaxies strut their stuff,
Plum-pudding supernovas, oh so buff!
Planetary pies spin in a dance,
While everyone joins in the chance!

Celestial Choreography

In outer space, the stars all dance,
With twinkling steps, they take a chance.
The comets swirl, they spin and glide,
While asteroids join, in a cosmic ride.

Neptune winks at playful Mars,
While Saturn's rings go 'round like cars.
A galaxy-wide ballet unfolds,
With all of them wearing sparkly golds.

A black hole whispers, 'Join the fun!',
As stardust struts, oh what a run!
Planets twirl in gravity's game,
Each one laughs, and none feels tame.

So grab your space shoes, don't be shy,
The universe beckons, let's all fly!
In this vast realm where laughter flows,
Dance like nobody cares, who knows?

Cosmic Rhythms Unveiled

In a nebula's hug, the space folks grin,
As meteors hop, and begin to spin.
Galactic giggles echo from afar,
While Pluto says, 'Hey, I'm still a star!'

Comets chase, like kids in the park,
With tails that glitter, they leave a mark.
The Milky Way snaps its fingers tight,
Creating beats that light up the night.

Shooting stars beam, like a dance flash,
Each wish sent up, makes a big splash.
Gravity pulls, but the joy is free,
Come join the fun, it's easy to see!

So laugh among planets, twirl and swirl,
With every orbit, give fate a whirl!
In this vast studio, let worries cease,
As we groove with the universe, full of peace.

Galactic Groove

Twirl through the cosmos, feel the beat,
With planets kicking up their feet.
Orions' belt ties the stars in a bow,
While Milky Way flows, just go with the flow.

Mercury runs, feeling quite spry,
While Jupiter jumps, reaching for the sky.
Uranus giggles, round and round,
As Venus serenades with a sweet sound.

Dancing space dust fills the air,
Echoes of laughter spin everywhere.
Time keeps ticking, but who really cares?
In this universe, fun freely shares.

So step to the left, and glide to the right,
The bigger the dream, the brighter the light.
Join this jig with a gleeful cheer,
In this cosmic dance, let joy persevere!

Star Trails and Twirling Tales

Follow the trails of stars in play,
Their silly antics light up the way.
Waves of giggles from galaxies afar,
As aliens jam on an air guitar.

Supernova throws a party so bright,
While black holes laugh, pulling in light.
Dancing around in shimmering space,
With meteors racing, keeping up the pace.

The universe twirls in a colorful spree,
Each axis spins with pure jubilee.
Asteroids clapping, a beat that rebounds,
As starlight hops with jubilant sounds.

So come on, earthlings, join the parade,
In this cosmic carnival, none are afraid.
Let's tap to the rhythm that nature conveys,
In twinkling harmony, we'll dance for days!

Beyond the Horizon of Tantalizing Tastes

In a land where flavors collide,
A cake with sprinkles, and stars won't hide.
Frosting waterfalls, oh what a scene,
Giant gumdrops rolling, like countless beans.

Lemons in jammies, lollipops cheer,
Marshmallow clouds, let's all grab a beer!
The whipped cream mountains, oh how they sway,
While jiggling jellyfish dance out to play.

Sassy cupcakes grin, with eyes made of gum,
They laugh as the donuts begin to hum.
With every bite, giggles galore,
Taste buds erupt, oh who could want more?

So come take a stroll on this sugary road,
Where every sweet step has a funny ode.
The horizon glimmers with tantalizing sights,
In this silly banquet, we reach new heights!

Radiant Revelations in the Cosmic Kitchen

In a kitchen where planets twirl and spin,
The pots are humming, let the laughter begin.
Who's making biscuits? It's Jupiter's task,
While Saturn stirs soup, with a sly little flask.

Neptune's fluffing pancakes with stardust sprinkles,
While Mars sneaks a taste and gives tiny winks.
All the aliens gather for a grand feast,
Sharing silly stories from the greatest to least.

A recipe from a comet, oh what a sight,
A pinch of starlight, to make it just right.
Galactic green beans, they wiggle and squawk,
As they leap from the pot with a silly little walk.

They serve up some laughter on plates made of stars,
As the Milky Way giggles, sharing sweet memoirs.
With every disclosure, there's joy all around,
In the cosmic kitchen, silliness abounds!

Galactic Stroll

As I walk through the cosmos, what do I see?
Planets in sneakers, racing with glee.
Stars buzzing by on their skateboard trails,
While moonbeams giggle and spin tiny tales.

Saturn does cartwheels, rings flying about,
While comets pass by with a query and shout.
'Hey Earth, do you fancy a game of tag?'
'Only if it's cosmic,' I cheer with a brag!

Through the cosmic park, a parade of delight,
Where suns wear sunglasses, shining so bright.
Asteroids play hopscotch, laughter so light,
In this galactic stroll, the vibes feel just right.

So join in the fun where gravity bends,
With a jubilant dance that never quite ends.
With every new step, absurdity reigns,
In this merry adventure, joy freely gains!

Celestial Dance in Stardust

In the ballroom of space, where the stardust twirls,
Planets in tuxedos, and comets in pearls.
Galactic greats gather, all set for a dance,
While the nebulae giggle, lost in a trance.

Supernova spins with a dazzling flare,
While black holes chuckle, with time to spare.
They sway to the rhythm of the universe's beat,
With laughter exploding, it's truly a treat.

Dancing on asteroids, they leap and they glide,
With each little wobble, they let joy guide.
The moons play tambourines, with a clang and a crash,
In this jolly celebration, they all make a splash.

So twirl in the stardust, let your spirit arise,
In this celestial dance, beneath twinkling skies.
For when laughter and joy join the cosmic ballet,
The universe chuckles, come dance, come play!

Ethereal Dances in the Sweet Abyss

Floating on marshmallow clouds,
The stars giggle, they're not too loud.
With sprinkles raining from the sky,
Silly whispers as we twirl high.

Jellybean rivers twist and sway,
Gummy bears join the ballet.
While chocolate comets zoom around,
Laughter echoes, a joyful sound.

Fudge fountains bubble, full of cheer,
Sugarplum fairies waltzing near.
In this space where sweets take flight,
We trip on cookies, what a sight!

Dance partners made of peanut cream,
We stumble through this candy dream.
Fluffy giggles and frosty glee,
In this abyss, we're wild and free.

Starry Pastries and Galactic Dreams

Dancing doughnuts in the night,
With icing stars, what a delight!
Jupiter's pies spin on a plate,
As we serve fun on a golden slate.

Brownies float like shooting stars,
In the glow of jelly jar bars.
We juggle cupcakes, fluffy and bright,
Swooping down, oh what a sight!

Crusty comets crossing paths,
With sugar sprinkles, we share laughs.
The Milky Way in whipped cream streams,
We dive into our sweetest dreams.

With each bite, a giggle bursts,
As frosted laughter fills our thirst.
In this banquet, we gleefully bask,
Under bright lights, what a sweet task!

Over the Moon with Sugar Delight

Bouncing high on whipped cream hills,
We chase the laughter, oh what thrills!
Sundae slides and taffy pulls,
Our sugar rush, it truly rules!

A gingerbread rocket, zooming fast,
With frosting trails that'll forever last.
We swing from licorice vines so sweet,
With silly treats beneath our feet.

Chocolate chips fall like starry rain,
Tasting our way through sugary gain.
With every giggle, another scoop,
We whirl and swirl in this sweet loop.

Puffed marshmallow clouds puff up high,
We dance beneath the taffy sky.
No one can resist this joyful flight,
Over the moon, what a sweet delight!

Celestial Sweets and Cosmic Beats

In a nebula of gummy bears,
We bounced and twirled without a care.
Twinkling tarts in every hue,
Swinging spoons like we're supposed to do.

Twirled around on frosting streams,
Floating high on sugary dreams.
Every laugh is a sprinkle song,
We're dancing where we all belong.

Moonbeam cakes and candy bars,
Under the glow of the candy stars.
What a party, oh what fun,
Savoring treats as we laugh and run.

With jelly shots that burst with cheer,
In this sweet space, we have no fear.
We spin and glide through this fleet,
Among celestial sweets, we feel complete!

Sweets of the Starry Night

Under the blanket of twinkling lights,
Chocolate rivers flow in delightful sights.
Marshmallow mountains, fluffy and round,
Jellybean critters bounce on the ground.

Whipped cream comets zoom past my face,
Gumdrops giggle in a sugary race.
Cupcake critters with sprinkles galore,
Dance on the pavement, always wanting more.

Astral Capers in Sugary Realms

Stars wear frosting, bright as the sun,
Licorice vines twist, oh what fun!
In candy-coated fields, we skip and play,
Where lollipop trees sway all day.

Bouncing gummy bears have quite the cheer,
Soda pop streams bubble near.
Syrupy sunbeams paint the ground,
In sugary worlds, laughter is found.

Cosmic Whirls of Frosted Dreams

Honeycombs whirl beneath dancing moons,
Frosted cookies hum sweet little tunes.
Candy canes twirl in harmonious glee,
While sour stars tease with giggles, you see.

Sundae rain falls in milky streams,
As jellyfish jiggle in whipped cream dreams.
Taffy tornadoes sweep us away,
In this wobbly whimsy, we eternally play.

Luminous Footsteps on Sugar Clouds

Up we leap on clouds made of fluff,
Where sugar rush turns giggles to puff.
Cotton candy trails lead the way,
To frosty delights where sunbeams play.

Flavors collide in a sweet parade,
As rainbow sprinkles dance, unafraid.
With our silly strides on this wobbly path,
We laugh through the flavors, sharing the math.

Symphonic Shadows of Space

In the void, where starlight plays,
Alien dancers spin and sway,
With wobbling legs and silly hats,
They soar and glide like friendly cats.

Comets race on marshmallow trails,
While giggling meteors share their tales,
Jupiter's balloons drift with glee,
In this wacky space jamboree.

Saturn's rings, a jester's crown,
Spinning round, they tumble down,
A wiggly worm in cosmic socks,
Shakes its groove 'neath stellar rocks.

So let us dance on nebula streets,
With twinkling stars as our upbeat beats,
In this jest, the universe chuckles,
As we stomp in space, and joy just snuggles.

Universe Unwound

Galaxies slip on their best shoes,
For a shuffle that'll leave you amused,
With laughing black holes, spinning around,
They leap through the depths, with no solid ground.

A solar flare joins the conga line,
Groovin' to sounds that twist and twine,
Neptune brings candy, an unexpected treat,
While Pluto plays maracas, oh so neat.

Stars throw confetti made of light,
While comets play tag in their joyful flight,
The Milky Way hums a whimsical song,
While time bends giggles, where we all belong.

In this unraveling dance of delight,
The universe sparkles, colorful and bright,
So twirl with the tides, spin with the dust,
And embrace the absurd, as we undoubtedly must.

Twinkling Trails of Heavenly Sweets

Stars sprinkle frosting on the night,
Galaxies dance in a sugary light.
Comets zip by with candy delight,
Laughter echoes in this joyful flight.

Floating marshmallows drift in the breeze,
Celestial sprinkles bring hearts to their knees.
With bites of stardust, we munch with glee,
In this feast of wonder, how sweet it can be.

Planets roll by on a jelly-like swirl,
Each twist and turn makes our taste buds twirl.
Nibbling on cookies that spin and twirl,
In this wacky world, our giggles unfurl.

So grab a spoon and dig in with flair,
Savor the flavors that fill up the air.
With each playful nibble, we're free as a dare,
In trails of sweetness, with joy we share.

Sugar Coated Adventures in the Void

In the belly of space, where sweetness flows,
  Candy-red asteroids sparkle and pose.
  Chocolates orbit, as laughter bestows,
  Floating among jellybeans in rows.

Candy clouds sprinkle with gumball rain,
Tickled by sugar, we dance through the gain.
With giggling galaxies that never constrain,
In this realm of frosting, we chuckle in vain.

Lollipop comets, oh what a delight,
  Zipping around in a sugary flight.
We ride on cookies, our hearts feeling light,
While tasting the stars that shimmer at night.

Adventure awaits in this playful abyss,
  Where every bite brings a sugary bliss.
  In the void, we munch, nothing's amiss,
With laughter that echoes, a cosmic sweet kiss.

Constellation Confections

Twinkling sweets in a night so profound,
Candy canes spiral, round and around.
Milkshake rivers bubble with sound,
In the cosmic kitchen, wonders abound.

Star-shaped pastries glide through the air,
While jelly-filled planets do a dance in their lair.
With sprinkles of joy, they twirl without care,
In this sweet galaxy, laughter we share.

Donuts with glaze shine like morning dew,
Floating in harmony, a joyful crew.
With cupcake clouds drifting, our dreams come true,
In the land of delights, there's always room for two.

So take a big bite of this tasty delight,
Where constellations bring flavor to light.
With each giggle shared, our hearts take flight,
In the realm of confections, happiness ignites.

Wanderlust in a Universe of Flavors

From milky ways made of creamy delight,
To cookie crumbles that give us a fright.
In layers of flavors, oh what a sight,
We skip through the cosmos on this sweet night.

Pies stargaze quietly, covered in cream,
Whipped toppings giggle as planets all beam.
Riding on waves of a frothy ice dream,
In this universe, nothing's quite as it seems.

Cakes spin like moons, with frosting so bright,
Layered in joy, such a glorious sight.
Bouncing between stars brings sheer delight,
In a world of flavors, all wrong turns feel right.

So pack up your taste buds, let's venture afar,
In a universe rich with each glorious star.
With laughter and joy, like a sweet candy bar,
We wander forever, where flavor is star.

Interstellar Dance of the Unknown

In a swirling galaxy of glee,
Stars twirl like they're on a spree.
With wobbly legs and bright red shoes,
They stumble and trip, but never lose.

Nebulae laugh as they join the fun,
Chasing black holes and light from the sun.
Planets roll in a wacky game,
Each one giggles, no one's to blame.

Comets whoosh with a playful cheer,
Leaving trails of laughter, never fear.
The universe winks, a mischievous smile,
Let's dance together, stay for a while.

In this vast space, we shuffle and prance,
Galactic beings join in the dance.
Who knew the stars had such a flair?
Come join the party, float in midair!

Starry Night's Ballet

Moonbeams stretch in glittering rows,
While twinkling stars steal the show.
Asteroids leap in graceful arcs,
With quirky rhythms, they leave their marks.

Meteorites spin, a dizzying sweep,
While aliens giggle, some solemnly peep.
A black hole winks, makes a joke about fate,
As space dust shuffles to a newfound state.

The Milky Way sways with all of its might,
Whispering secrets deep in the night.
Dancing in circles, a starry brigade,
In this cosmic ballet, none are afraid.

Through comets' tails, we float and glide,
In this stellar amphitheater, we take pride.
Laughter resonates, a soft, gentle tune,
Underneath the glow of a friendly moon.

Celestial Boundaries and Floating Dreams

In the realms where stardust scatters wide,
Galactic giggles and dreams collide.
Nebulous wonders twirling about,
With whimsical feasts; who knows what's out?

Floating islands of joy drift by,
As planets munch on space apple pie.
Uranus spins, but who can tell?
If it's laughter or just a starry spell.

Traveling light with a bounce in our step,
Gravity's a myth; we just adept.
Jovial forces guide every sway,
In the dance of the dreamers, we find our way.

Through cosmic realms, we'll wander and fret,
Collecting odd things, no need to fret.
Each twinkling light, a chuckle or beam,
In the expanse where we laugh and dream.

Pulsar's Polka

A pulsar spins with a tock and a tick,
Its rhythm contagious, comes in a flick.
With twinkling flares and a jolly beat,
Stars shake their bodies, tapping their feet.

Jupiter plays with a trumpet's boom,
While Saturn twirls in its glittery plume.
Neptune's blowing bubbles, oh what a sight!
A symphony of laughter lights up the night.

Even dark matter wants in on the scene,
Wiggling and squiggling, a sight so keen.
Every quasar joins in, part of the crew,
Twirling and swirling in bright cosmic hue.

So let's join the polka, spin 'round the star,
With friends in the twilight, we'll dance near and far.
In pulsating joy, we'll celebrate play,
In this vibrant universe, come dance and sway!

Cosmic Treadmill of Time

On a treadmill spinning, we race in glee,
Stars in their sneakers, can you feel the spree?
Gravity's a prankster, it pulls us around,
While wishes are joggers that dance on the ground.

Planets are laughing, it's quite the machine,
Swinging their orbits in loops that are keen.
We tripped over comets, rolled past the moons,
A celestial cardio to some funky tunes.

Eons are fleeting, yet somehow we glide,
Running through ages, with friends side by side.
Time takes a tumble, while we skip and sway,
In this groovy workout, we laugh all the way.

So lace up your stardust, jump on the track,
Forget all your worries, there's no looking back.
With a hop and a skip, let's make our own fate,
In this cosmic gym, let's levitate!

Universal Sidewalk Symphony

On cosmic sidewalks where echoes collide,
Planets perform as they twist and they slide.
Jupiter jives with a rhythm so grand,
While Saturn grooves with a ringside band.

Stars are the streetlamps, shining so bright,
Dancing their tune in the soft, starry night.
We prance with the comets, in lanes made of light,
As space winds up for a galactic delight.

Uranus twerks with its whimsical flair,
While Mars offers beats from its disco lair.
Together we twirl, in a joyous parade,
This quirky ballet that the cosmos has made.

So join in the shuffle, don't miss the fun,
Where laughter and music unite everyone.
In this universal groove, we'll echo and sway,
As the stars sing along to our bright cabaret!

Nebula Night's Out

Under a blanket of shimmering dust,
Nebulae gather, it's a starlit must.
With colors like candy, they twirl and they spin,
In this festive ballet, everyone wins!

Let's paint the cosmos in pops of delight,
Each swirl a giggle, a burst of pure light.
We'll dance with the clouds, all fluffy and bright,
While meteors rock out, oh what a sight!

Constellations are cheering, it's all quite bizarre,
As we groove through the night, under each shining star.
We've brought snacks from Earth: asteroids and cake,
Nibbling on laughter—oh, for goodness' sake!

So swing through the nebulae, giggle and shout,
With every twinkling star, there's no room for doubt.
This night will be cosmic, a whimsical blend,
In the nebula dreamy where fun has no end!

Astral Adventure Through the Cosmos

Let's embark on a ride through the stellar expanse,
With comets like taxis, inviting a dance.
We'll buckle up time in our spaceship of light,
And soar through the galaxies, oh what a sight!

We zoom past the suns that are baking some pies,
While Martians are serving up cosmic fries.
We'll hop over rings, and the moons that applaud,
In this crazy adventure, a journey untawed.

The black holes are portals to giggles and cheer,
Transporting us swiftly, there's nothing to fear.
On stardust highways, we're laughing so loud,
This astral escapade—come join the crowd!

So pack up your joy, let your worries take flight,
In this raucous adventure, everything feels right.
With each cosmic turn, there's a surprise that awaits,
We'll dance through the universe, celebrating fates!

Cosmic Jamboree of Dreams

In a world where stars wear shoes,
Planets dance with silly moves,
Galaxies grin with balmy glee,
While comets juggle cups of tea.

Bouncing moons in polka dots,
Whirlwinds pull out crazed robots,
Shooting stars play hide and seek,
As asteroids sigh, "Let's be cheeky!"

Naughty nebulae twirl and spin,
With twinkling lights, they pull you in,
Laughter echoes in the void,
Quantum quirks, we all enjoyed!

Swinging through the orbs of night,
Tickling tails with sheer delight,
Come along, don't be too shy,
In dreamland where the wacky fly.

Celestial Carousel

Round and round the bright stars twirl,
Planets giggle, flinging pearls,
Saturn's rings are hoops of fun,
While Venus winks at everyone!

Zany rockets zoom and glide,
Moonbeams serve a joyful ride,
Silly aliens join the race,
Chasing stardust, a merry chase!

Twirling comets in a row,
Frolicking in the starry glow,
Wobbly asteroids laugh and shout,
As space explorers dance about!

Spinning tales of cosmic cheer,
Jolly laughter, drawing near,
Grab a friend, let's laugh and swirl,
On this merry-go-round of pearls!

Constellation Capers

Hercules lifts his silly cap,
While Orion takes a nap,
Pleiades play with glowing knacks,
As Gemini cracks silly quacks.

Leo roars with joyful flare,
And Virgo spins without a care,
A parrot stars and meteors sing,
In the show, it's a wild fling!

Laughter bounces through the sky,
As playful shadows whirl and fly,
Twirling through the starry page,
Each glow, a quirky cosmic stage!

Join the jesters in their play,
In the universe, fun's the way,
Giggles shared among the stars,
In this vast, majestic bazaar!

Milky Way Masquerade

Dressed in stardust, planets prance,
Winking at the moonlit dance,
Comets wear their best bow ties,
As they twirl beneath the skies.

Stars swap hats and wink with glee,
Meteors play party marquee,
Jupiter's gaff-tape gets unstuck,
As Saturn rolls—Oh, what a luck!

Neon nebulae paint in style,
With colors bright that make you smile,
Each twinkle holds a joke or two,
As moonbeams join the crazy crew!

So grab a partner, dance away,
In this wild celestial fray,
With laughter echoing through space,
Join the masquerade—what a grace!

Stellar Strolls Amongst Celestial Confections

In a realm where sweets take flight,
Bright candies twinkle, what a sight!
Gummy stars with laughter burst,
Sugar comets, oh how they thirst!

Jelly beans on marshmallow hills,
Dancing lightly, giving thrills.
Chocolate rivers flowing fast,
Every step a giggle cast.

Lollipop trees sway and sway,
Humming tunes, they want to play.
Whipped cream clouds in skies of blue,
Join the party; there's room for you!

So grab your friends, let's take a ride,
On candy moons, we'll laugh and slide.
With each bounce, a sugary sound,
In this sweet dreamland, joy is found!

Galactic Pastries in the Sky

In this universe of treats divine,
We find pastries that simply shine.
Asteroid cakes with sprinkles bright,
Sugar dustings take to flight!

Donut planets roll and spin,
Pastry fun is where we begin.
Flaky croissants with a twist,
Amongst the stars, they coexist.

Cupcake comets flash and dart,
Creating sweetness, heart to heart.
Tarts shaped like the lovely moon,
Join together to play a tune!

Take a bite, let laughter rise,
With every taste, see joyful eyes.
In a bakery among the stars,
Let's dance and munch—who needs guitars?

Dancing on the Edges of Deep Space

In the void, where giggles reign,
We shimmy past with joy, no strain.
Floating cookies, round they go,
With every twirl, their sprinkles glow.

Moon pies bounce on hidden swings,
As peanut butter sings and sings.
Fizzy drinks in cosmic cheer,
We step and twirl without a fear.

Brownie asteroids in a race,
With icing trails, they set the pace.
Doughnut stars in dazzling rows,
Finding laughter where joy flows.

Join the dance, it's quite the spree,
In this starry galaxy.
With every step, we share delight,
In the vastness, it feels so right!

The Milky Way Bakery

Welcome to the world of treats!
Where every flavor playfully meets.
Cupcakes swirl like nebulae,
In buttery bliss, we float and fly.

Brownie bites wrapped like a hug,
In chocolate love, they softly snug.
Doughy delights, fresh from the press,
Filling our hearts with sheer happiness.

Candy comets zoom by fast,
In sugary trails of joy amassed.
Biscuits and pies, a wondrous sight,
In this sweet haven, all feels right.

So gather 'round, don't be shy,
In this bakery, we touch the sky.
With every munch, a giggle shared,
In our cosmic kitchen, love is prepared!

The Great Beyond's Ballet

In the vast expanse where the stars do twirl,
A dancing comet gives a wink and a whirl.
Nebulous clouds form the stage's delight,
While black holes giggle, pulling all things tight.

Planets prance in their orbits so round,
With Saturn's rings letting laughter abound.
Asteroids shuffle in wacky, wild glee,
As Martians toast to their galactic spree.

Stardust sprinkled like confetti they fling,
As the sun beams down to join in the swing.
Jupiter jumps with a bounce so absurd,
While flaming meteors twirl, tails blurred.

The Milky Way's groove is a sight to behold,
With secrets of laughter in stories retold.
In this ballet of wonders, one can't help but grin,
As the universe chuckles in a whimsical spin.

Secrets of the Starry Stage

Under the glow of the moon's silly face,
Stars gather 'round in a giggling race.
With twinkling eyes, they dazzle and play,
Whispers of humor light up the ballet.

Comets with capes do a spin and a slide,
While meteors shimmy in a celestial ride.
Dancing in rhythm, they frolic and glide,
Creating a symphony, joyous and wide.

Black holes chuckle, pulling stardust near,
While aliens juggle with zeroes and cheer.
A ballet of mischief in every bright wink,
As galaxies waltz on the edge of a pink.

Each star has a secret, a joke in its glow,
Of how the vast universe puts on a show.
With laughter that bounces across the great void,
In the cosmic performance, delight is deployed.

Galactic Footwork

Space-time contorts with a rhythm so strange,
Where galaxies shuffle and partners exchange.
Asteroids step with a tap-tap-tap,
While quarks do the twist in a funky mishap.

Neutron stars spin in a dazzling display,
Creating a whirlpool where dancers can play.
Wormholes giggle, twisting space into fun,
As they pull in a comet just for the run.

In the zany arena where starlight does beam,
Saturn's rings wiggle like a part of the dream.
Celestial footsteps leave trails made of glee,
As the cosmos jives with a jubilee spree.

A supernova's burst, a flash in the night,
All add to the spectacle of laughter and light.
So kick off your shoes, join the galactic spree,
With each merry step, let your worries all flee.

Universal Dance of Delight

In the grand ballroom where stardust does twine,
Planets all sway in a dance so divine.
Shooting stars leap with a flick and a whirl,
As cosmic confetti begins to unfurl.

Galaxies giggle with spirals of flair,
While quasars boogie in the cool, dark air.
Venus and Mars take a two-step in sync,
Sharing their secrets over a comet's wink.

Nebulas swirl, making colors collide,
Their hues bring bursts of joy worldwide.
In this universal dance, laughter prevails,
As humor takes center stage, leaving bright trails.

So sway with the rhythm of infinity's flow,
As the universe chuckles in every bright glow.
Kick up your feet, let your spirit ignite,
In this comic ballet that stretches the night.

Frosted Footprints Across Time and Space

Twinkling sprinkles in a swirl,
The universe does a joyful twirl.
Stars are cookies, bright and round,
Bouncing in orbits, up and down.

Galaxies dance on frosting lanes,
While comets sing in candy canes.
Each planet spins with lemon zest,
As cake slices float, it's quite the fest!

Rolling through this doughy delight,
Asteroids laugh in sheer delight.
We hop on stardust spritzed with cheer,
Sharing giggles with the cosmos here.

So grab a bite, don't be shy,
In this absurdity, let's amplify.
Life's a dessert, let's take our place,
With frosted footprints, we race through space!

Orbital Treats in the Galactic Fair

Cotton candy clouds above us sway,
As we munch on stardust, hooray!
Galactic stands with pies and tarts,
Made from the sweetest cosmic arts.

Moons serve milkshakes in funky hues,
While black holes offer chocolate views.
Uranus spins with frosted flair,
While Saturn's rings are minty rare.

Gravitational pulls of jelly beans,
Floating through our vibrant dreams.
Space-time folds into a treat,
With laughter echoing, oh so sweet!

So grab a ticket, join the race,
To find delight in endless space.
This gala's joy will never end,
With orbital treats, we all transcend!

Spectral Delights in the Nebula

In the heart of clouds that twinkle bright,
Gummy bears dance in glowing light.
Rainbow ribbons swirl in glee,
Cosmic cake is served with tea!

Orion offers biscuits galore,
As Martian muffins hit the floor.
Life is sweet in this nebula,
Each bite a dream, a new fella!

Sprinkled stars on every plate,
Lunar popsicles, wait! Don't hesitate.
Step right up for a wild bite,
As laughter echoes through the night.

We'll tickle the void with joyful sounds,
Creating happiness all around.
In this realm of tasty shimmer,
The fun of flavors only gets dimmer!

Starlit Serenade of Gourmet Wonders

Under stars that play a tune,
Gourmet dreams come out at noon.
Whipped cream clouds, a frosted sky,
In this feast, we can't deny!

Cakes that rise like planetary spheres,
Chocolate rivers hide our fears.
Baking magic all around,
With fruity melodies abound.

We sing with shooting stars tonight,
As savory bites take flight.
Galactic soups with a twinkling laugh,
Joy spills over like a bubbling calf!

So let's waltz on milky ways,
In this banquet, we will play.
Embrace the wonders, munch with glee,
In this starlit serenade, we're free!

Treading the Milky Way

Stars twinkle in a frosty dance,
Glimmers of laughter, take a chance.
Floating past with giggles pure,
In zero gravity, we're sure!

Planets spin like wobbly tops,
Each moon a partner, never stops.
With every bounce and silly glide,
We tumble through the galaxy wide.

Asteroids roll, a fun surprise,
Be nimble now, oh how they fly!
A comet zips with a cheeky grin,
As we dodge around, let the fun begin!

In the vastness where we play,
Joyful hearts will find a way.
With every leap and spin we take,
The universe smiles, make no mistake!

Celestial Steps and Solar Swirls

Step by step on Solar beams,
Dancing through celestial dreams.
Whirls of light in colors bright,
We twist and turn, oh what a sight!

Jupiter swings, rings all aglow,
As we pass by, we put on a show.
With each turn, the stars do cheer,
In this vast ball, there's no fear!

Shooting stars like confetti rain,
We laugh and swirl, in joy we gain.
Galaxies shimmer with a wink,
In this fun dance, we hardly think!

With asteroid hops, we take our flight,
Through cosmic realms, what sheer delight!
In spirals of laughter, we twine and swerve,
With silly moves, we've got the verve!

Galactic Reverie

In the depths of night, we glide,
Stars our friends, they're on our side.
With a hop and a skip, we'd sway,
In this dance, let's shout hooray!

Nebulas swirl with colors bold,
Sprinkling joy like tales of old.
With every twirl, we'll spin and sway,
In harmony, we'll laugh away.

Comets race, what a game we play,
Zooming 'round in a merry sway.
Each little planet giggles too,
Under this sky, there's room for two!

In this dream, where all is light,
We laugh and twirl throughout the night.
In the dance of stars and moon's embrace,
In a kooky world, we find our place!

Intergalactic Improvisation

Jazz hands on a shooting star,
We groove and jig, we've come so far.
With every beam, we strut our style,
In the vastness, let's make a smile!

Planets join in, a funky beat,
Their orbits jive and can't be beat.
With cosmic rhythms all around,
We bounce along, no need for ground!

In this space where laughter reigns,
We kick and spin, oh what fun gains.
No routine here, we make it up,
In whimsical steps, we twirl and sup!

So grab a friend from distant skies,
And dance until we fill the ties.
In stellar joy, let's play all night,
In intergalactic thrills, pure delight!

Starry Strolls and Sonic Waves

In velvet skies we tiptoe bright,
With giggles echoing in the night.
Stars are winking, what a scene!
As laughter dances in between.

Sonic waves we surf so high,
Tickling clouds, oh my, oh my!
We slide on beams of moonlit grace,
In this cheeky, starry place.

Infinite Waltz of the Universe

Round and round, the worlds do twirl,
Like a dizzy dance, they spin and swirl.
Galaxies giggle, planets play,
In this grand ballet, come what may.

With comets trailing behind their tails,
They join the fun in cosmic trails.
And when they blast, like confetti rain,
The universe chuckles, never in vain.

Aurora's Cosmic Waltz

At dawn, the auroras paint the sky,
With colors that wink and flutter by.
They shimmy and shake in frosty air,
   A cosmic dance without a care.

With every twist, and every turn,
Stars above spin and brightly burn.
Whispers of laughter fill the night,
   In this striking, colorful light.

Nebula Nights and Distant Lights

In the nebula's glow, we hop and play,
Chasing the stardust that floats our way.
With each spark, a joke is born,
Laughter ripples through the dawn.

Distant lights twinkle in a wink,
Making us giggle, just stop and think.
Every wink from the stars we catch,
Adds to the joy, what a perfect match!

Stardust Trails

In a universe where the comets play,
They juggle moons in a galactic ballet.
Shooting stars drop pies from the night sky,
While aliens laugh as they twirl by.

Gravity's low, and the giggles rise,
Beaming beams from their curious eyes.
With every leap, they make a wish,
Floating donuts? Oh, what a dish!

They dance on asteroids, round and round,
While planets chant without a sound.
A parade of shapes, in awkward grace,
Each twirl brings smiles, each jump a chase.

In this meteor shower of joy and delight,
The universe sparkles; it's quite a sight.
So grab a friend, let your spirit fly,
In this wacky fest, we'll reach for the sky!

Cosmic Horizons and Planetary Pirouettes

Planets spin with a funky beat,
While space cats tap their tiny feet.
Galaxies twist with a giggly grace,
Bouncing around in a whirlwind space.

Uranus winks, and Neptune spins,
A dance-off under the cosmic winds.
With swirling skirts made of starlit flow,
They flaunt their moves, stealing the show!

Saturn sways with a hula hoop ring,
While Martians strum on a space-age string.
Jupiter jumps, making everyone sway,
In this planetary party, come join the fray!

Each orbit, a laugh, a twinkle, a cheer,
In the cosmic dance hall, there's nothing to fear.
From whimsical worlds, laughter takes flight,
In the endless expanse, what a joy! What a night!

Etheric Duet Under the Stars

Two comets chase across the twilight,
Singing tunes that feel just right.
With twinkling rhythms and playful beats,
They waltz through halos of moonlit streets.

Their tails sway low, a shimmering show,
As planets join in, all aglow.
With giggles echoing through the expanse,
They invite the stars to join in the dance.

"Round and round," the nebulae cheer,
As cosmic critters gather near.
With stardust confetti raining down,
Every leap sprinkles joy around!

In this etheric duet, the night's alive,
With all of space, they hope to thrive.
Hilarity rises with each fleeting star,
As laughter rings out from near and far!

Constellation's Lullaby

In a sky of dreams where the puppets twirl,
The unicorns prance in a starlit whirl.
Gentle whispers from Orion's bow,
Mythical creatures dance to the glow.

A turtle winks from the Great Bear's might,
While dragons sip tea, it's quite the sight!
With every giggle, the Milky Way grins,
As constellations spin like joyful twins.

The Pleiades hum a sweet, funny tune,
As asteroids zoom past the smiling moon.
Galactic giggles echo in silence,
While the universe chuckles at its own brilliance.

So close your eyes, let dreams take flight,
To this lullaby under the starlit night.
In cosmic vastness, the laughter we weave,
In the arms of the stars, forever believe!

Dancing Shadows of Light

In the glow of stars so bright,
Moonbeams twirl in a silly fight,
Jupiter laughs with pearly grace,
While comets join the frolic space.

Galaxies spin in a joyful spree,
Asteroids wink, oh can you see?
Planets play hopscotch in a line,
Singing tunes that feel divine.

The sun wears shades, a radiant hue,
With every flip, a cosmic view,
Gravity plays a funky bass,
As stars twinkle at a dizzy pace.

In this dance, all worries fade,
Each twirl is a joke that's handmade,
With laughter echoing through the night,
In shadows that dance, oh what a sight!

Wandering Through Celestial Paths

On paths where stardust sneakers glide,
Aliens jive with laughter and pride,
Silly satellites sip cosmic tea,
Chasing tails of shooting stars with glee.

Planets whisper secrets so bold,
While black holes welcome tales retold,
Quasars flicker like fireflies bright,
Creating humor in the endless night.

Freestyle comets dodge and dart,
Each orbit a burst of cosmic art,
Meteor showers play hide-and-seek,
Tickling the universe, cheek to cheek.

Under the veil of a starry dome,
We dance among the endless foam,
With giggles swirling around our feet,
In a cosmic race that feels so sweet!

Orbital Elegance

In graceful arcs, the stars do prance,
With moons in gowns, they take a chance,
A waltz with planets, round they go,
To rhythms only space would know.

Saturn twirls with rings so fine,
And Venus laughs, feeling divine,
Neptune spins with a splash of blue,
While the Milky Way sings out, woohoo!

Twinkling lights join in the fun,
Each orbit, a race that's never done,
Astrophysics in a spin, so chic,
A dazzling display of cosmic streaks.

Beneath this canopy, we dance along,
With laughter echoing like a song,
As gravity leads with a gentle sway,
In this elegant ballet, we laugh and play.

Gravity's Gentle Sway

In a field of stars, we sway and twirl,
With gravity's hug, we whirl and whirl,
A gentle tug, a playful tease,
As planets pop like dancing peas.

With each leap, the cosmos beams,
As we float through space like silly dreams,
Nebulae giggle, a colorful sight,
Turning stardust into pure delight.

Asteroids dance, a clumsy cheer,
Gravity's pull makes them adhere,
Wobbly orbits, a two-step chase,
As galaxies giggle in this wide embrace.

So let's spin with a cosmic grin,
With joy that bubbles from within,
In this dance of celestial play,
Where laughter follows, come what may!

Lunar Waltz Through the Nebula

Bouncing on craters, oh what a sight,
While aliens giggle, dancing in flight.
Moon pies are tossed, with a splash of good cheer,
As comets join in, bringing laughter so near.

Galactic DJs spin tunes from afar,
With Saturn's rings shining like a bizarre star.
We jiggle and wiggle, in zero-grav bliss,
In this celestial soirée, who could resist?

Stars tease and twirl, all wearing bright hats,
A squirrel in a spacesuit, now how about that?
Jupiter winks with a mischievous plan,
While Mars rolls a ball, in this dreamy space span.

With a wink and a nod, the universe sighs,
Grooving together beneath starlit skies.
What a wild ride, our feet start to ache,
But we dance and we laugh, oh, the joy of the wake!

Interstellar Stride

A hop through the cosmos, we sway with delight,
Banana peels scatter, it's a wacky night.
Space kittens bounce in their neon-lit suits,
While goofy green Martians play banjo on flutes.

Shooting stars zoom like a zany parade,
As we boogie with meteors, no plans made.
In each leap and shuffle, we giggle and grin,
Floating through starlight, let the fun begin!

Milky Way twinkling, a dance for the bold,
Alien dance-offs, stories retold.
With every wild move, laughter fills the air,
An interstellar jig that you just can't compare.

So join in the shuffle, let your troubles drift,
As we waltz among planets, oh what a gift!
In this fancy footwork, we lose track of time,
In the vastness of space, we dance on a dime!

Starlit Serenade

With twinkling lights, we gather 'round,
To hear the sweet beats from the void profound.
The sun strums a tune, with rays so bright,
As stars hum along in the shimmering night.

Dancing on Saturn, we stomp and we sway,
With goofy galactic moves, hip-hip-hooray!
Space bears in tuxedos serve cookies and cake,
In this festive affair, oh, what joy to partake!

Comets are spinning, with glitter and flair,
While asteroids waltz with a debonair air.
Each leap is a giggle, each twirl is a cheer,
As the universe grins from deep atmosphere.

Round and around, the cosmos does spin,
With laughter and music, let the night begin!
In this starlit jaunt, together we gleam,
Woven in whimsy, like a whimsical dream!

Aurora's Gentle Glide

Across the great void, we sway and twirl,
With flashing colors that spin and whirl.
The auroras giggle, as we float on sighs,
Painting the dark with bright, joyful ties.

Dancing with planets, we glide through the night,
In a waltz with the stars, everything feels right.
As meteors dash and waves of light play,
We joyfully frolic in a ballet of rays.

Here comes a spaceship, with music so sweet,
A funky space band making hearts skip a beat.
With each delicious laugh, the universe beams,
In this cosmic ballet, we dance through our dreams.

So pass me a star, let's add to the fun,
As we swirl through the cosmos, under the sun.
With silly little spins, we'll never collide,
In this glowing parade, where joy is our guide!

Space Walk at Dusk

Floating in the sky so high,
With rubber boots and a silly tie.
Waving at the stars that grin,
Let the wacky show begin!

Bouncing off the moon's bright face,
While comets join the goofy race.
A galactic trampoline in sight,
Wobbling left and bouncing right!

Planetary parties with snacks to share,
Alien hosts in feathered flair.
Sipping starlight through a straw,
What a silly cosmic law!

As dusk descends, we twirl and spin,
In a waltz of giggles, let the fun begin.
With every leap, the stars all cheer,
For this is the spacewalk of the year!

Dancing Among the Celestial Bodies

In a twist of fate, we swirl and sway,
Pirouetting through the Milky Way.
Jupiter's grooving, oh what a sight,
While Mars joins in, with all its might!

Asteroids shimmy, asteroids shake,
Making sure the dance floor won't break.
With cosmic beats from a supernova,
We're grooving like a funky sofa!

Twinkling stars flash their silly lights,
While Saturn wobbles, oh what delights!
Kicking up stardust, we spin and glide,
In this dance of planets, we take great pride!

No gravity here, just endless fun,
As we dance until the break of sun.
With all the galaxies in our troupe,
We laugh together in a cosmic loop!

Echoes of the Void

In the silence, a giggle creeps,
From the shadows where nothing sleeps.
Echoes of laughter bounce around,
In the void, a funny sound!

An argument with a black hole spins,
Claiming it stole my favorite pins.
'Hey, you can't suck me in,' I chant,
As it chuckles, like a cosmic plant!

Nebulas hosting a raucous show,
Sprinkling confetti, oh what a glow!
Each twinkle whispers a silly tale,
As I dance on the tail of a comet's trail!

Bantering with stars, all in bright cheer,
In this void, there's nothing to fear.
With jokes that echo through space so wide,
Let's giggle together in this cosmic ride!

Stardust Canvas

Drawing outlines on a darkened sky,
With crayons made from a shooting star fly.
Every line giggles, a masterpiece bright,
As I sketch the planets with pure delight!

Brush strokes of nebulae swirl and twirl,
Creating fun shapes that giggle and whirl.
Oh look, a smiley face on the moon,
Wink at the sun, let's dance to a tune!

Painting with laughter, colors of glee,
The universe winks back at me.
While swirling in stardust, we stomp and jive,
Creating a canvas where joy comes alive!

As comets help splash colors galore,
The giggles of space we simply can't ignore.
With every stroke, the cosmos agrees,
Art and laughter flow on the galactic breeze!

www.ingramcontent.com/pod-product-compliance
Lightning Source LLC
Chambersburg PA
CBHW051635160426
43209CB00004B/663